Published in Great Britain 1996
by Bloomsbury Children's Books
2 Soho Square, London W1V 6HB

Text copyright © Peter Hoggarth 1996

Illustrations by Woody
Edited by Mike Hirst
Cover design by AB3
Text design by Louise Millar

A CIP record for this book is available from the British Library.

ISBN 0 7475 2686 9

Printed and bound in Great Britain by
Cox & Wyman, Reading, Berkshire

10 9 8 7 6 5 4 3 2 1

ROAR!

Animal Rights
Handbook for Kids

by Peter Hoggarth

Illustrations by Woody

INTRODUCTION:
REASONS TO ROAR

Humans are just one of the millions of animal species alive on planet Earth today. Sadly for the other living things – from lions, elephants and whales to cats, cows and earwigs – we're not always the best of neighbours.

We hunt animals, steal their fur, eat them, destroy their homes and, worst of all, even accuse some of them of being ugly! Imagine the low self-esteem poor old spiders must have after years of humans going 'Eek!' every time they see one.

Circus animals, hunted foxes and hairy bathroom spiders can't really club together and say, 'We're fed up with the way humans behave', so it's up to us – the two-legged, non-furry animals – to look after them. Welcome to animal rights!

In this book you'll find a campaigning-crusading, pet-walking, nature-reserving, petition-signing, anti-hunting, vivisection-debating, letter-writing, wildlife-saving, factory-farm-investigating, vegetarian-cooking world of animal-friendly action. You'll soon realize just what you can do, and that a trip to the shops or a letter to your MP can help animal rights just as much as the biggest and most expensive government projects.

And remember . . . next time you see a spider, no matter how hairy or huge, don't squash it!

CONTENTS

1 Here Today – Gone Tomorrow!   8

2 Old MacDonald Had a Farm   17

3 Blood Sports: A Blot on the Landscape?   27

4 Animals in the Lab   39

5 Zoos: Conservation or Cruelty?   50

6 The Animal Entertainment Swindle   59

7 Creature Comforts – Pets at Home   67

8 Going Veggie   76

9 Carry on Campaigning   91

One
HERE TODAY –
GONE TOMORROW!

Imagine a not-too distant future . . . There are no wild animals left! Terry Nutkins and David Attenborough are out of a job. No swinging monkeys, grooving gorillas or rocking rhinos.

Could this nightmare ever really happen? It's possible, because today species are becoming extinct 1,000 times faster than before humans appeared on planet Earth. It's high time we gave our fellow creatures a break.

Why is it Happening?

Lots of reasons. Number one is that humans have upset Mother Nature's natural balance and are bulldozing their way through animal habitats at a head-spinning rate.

Disappearing Rainforests Half of all the different species on Earth live in tropical rainforests, yet every second an area the size of a football pitch disappears. The trees are used as raw materials (for wood and paper) and the land is then used for cattle and crops.

Hunting is another big problem. Many animals are endangered because they are killed for their fur or skins. Snakes shed their skins naturally (luckily for them) but most other animals don't. A tiger can't just buy a new coat in the winter sales.

Crocodile Shoes Some people think they'll be a snappier dresser by wearing crocodile-skin shoes. Crocodiles, however, do not share this opinion.

Going, Going, Gone?

Nellie the elephant would certainly pack her trunk if she saw her ivory tusks used to make ornaments. Rhinoceroses would be on the run, too, if they knew that their horns might be used to make quack medicines. And what about the gorillas who are in danger of being served up as ape steak and chips in some African restaurants?

Humans have already made hundreds of species extinct – as dead as a dodo in fact (but that's another story . . .) Here are a few species still struggling for survival. Find out about your fave furry friends, and fill in a checklist like this one to keep a close eye on how they're doing.

SPECIES	ESTIMATED NO. IN THE WILD	MAIN THREAT
Giant Panda	1,000	Lost habitats, hunting.
Sumatran Rhino	200	Hunting.
Madagascan Fish Eagle	30 pairs	Lost habitats, hunting.
Koala Bears	A few thousand	Lost habitats, hunting.

Humans have made some animals disappear, but with a little magic (and common sense), hey presto, we can help surviving species to reappear. Welcome to . . .

Operation Tiger Not a 007-style spy story, but a concerted effort to save the tiger from extinction. Until recently, the tiger was one of the most threatened animals on Earth.

Then, in 1972, Operation Tiger was started by the Indian government and the WWF (Worldwide Fund for Nature). They set up tiger reserves where hunting was banned and tigers could breed. Today, tigers are no longer heading for Number One spot in the endangered species hit parade. It's grrrrrreat!

TIGER RESERVE.

What Can You Do?

Simple enough:
- Don't ever buy ivory or fur.
- Next time your parents buy new furniture, remember that teak, ebony, rosewood and mahogany look better in the rainforest. Or ask if the wood came from a sustainable forest (i.e. a forest where new trees are planted when the old ones are chopped down).
- Adopt an animal. Don't worry, you won't have to share your bedroom with a hippo – you can conveniently sponsor an animal in the wild.

Two organizations who can tell you more are:

BORN FREE FOUNDATION
Cherry Tree Cottage,
Coldharbour, Dorking,
Surrey RH5 6HA

SUSTAINABLE FOREST.

WWF
Panda House, Weyside Park,
Godalming,
Surrey GU7 1XR

Meanwhile, Closer to Home . . .

Exotic creatures aren't the only animals in danger.
There's work to be done protecting species at home too.
Just think, wolves used to be native animals of Britain,
but they became extinct during the reign of Henry VIII
(so did two of his wives!)

Hidden Danger Crops
sprayed with pesticides may
stop insects from munching
through cornfields before you
get your cornflakes, but they
can do more harm than good.
Birds of prey who eat rodents
who have themselves eaten
pesticide poisons may end up
becoming 'as sick as a parrot'.

Litter is a more direct
danger. Curious animals
might swallow rubbish, or get
stuck in it or strangled by it.
Don't be a litter bug.

13

Take A Walk on the Wild Side You'll have plenty of feathered friends if you build a bird table in your garden or put out bird feeders. Visitors will just flock to you!

Fish ponds They will attract a whole kingdom of minibeasts to your back garden.

Conservation for the Preservation of our Nature Reservations Action time! Why not find out if a local nature reservation could use your help? Or you could join a conservation group and help to transform wasteland into animal habitats.

More Trees, Please!

Did you know that up to 284 species of insect can live in a single oak tree.

There's not enough room to swing a centipede in here!

But woods are disappearing fast, and they're being replaced by motorways and other developments quicker than you can say 'Watford Gap'.

Crazy Campaigns In some campaigns, people have actually taken to the trees and cohabited with the squirrels in order to save woodland habitats from being destroyed. On one hillside in Sussex campaigners created a huge, eye-catching chalk figure to draw attention to a proposed road scheme. On a more down-to-earth level, the environmental pressure group Friends of the Earth rallied support to stop plans to widen the M25 motorway. Public pressure forced the scheme to be scrapped. Hooray!

Start Scribbling!

You don't have to swing through the trees or wrestle bulldozers if your favourite forest is under threat of becoming a concrete jungle. You can show your opposition by writing to your MP and saying (politely, of course), 'Your new road scheme is BONKERS!'

Perhaps something like this:

> Miss Theresa Green,
> 40 Oak Drive,
> Pineford,
> Nottinghampshire
>
> Mr Ivor Bypass,
> House of Commons,
> London SW1A OAA
>
> Dear Mr Bypass,
> I am writing to tell you about my opposition to the plans to widen the M666 near Pineford. I believe that it will only add to pollution and traffic congestion in our district, and will also destroy a great deal of local wildlife.
>   I would be grateful if you would reconsider your support for this road scheme, and look forward to hearing from you.
>
> Yours sincerely,
>
> Theresa Green

PS. It doesn't help if you threaten not to vote for your MP in the next election if you're not old enough!

Two
OLD MACDONALD HAD A FARM

Do you ever ponder what's happening on that farm over yonder? It might not be a happy green scene of jolly farmers murmuring 'ooo-aargh' while sheep graze peacefully in green pastures.

Nowadays, many farms are more like factories. In go chickens, pigs and cows. Out come nuggets, sausages and bacon.

Factory farming is about making money – by rearing as many animals in as little space as possible. Wildlife may be endangered but in Britain cows and their farmyard friends outnumber humans by three to one.

So read on . . . it's time to meet the meat you eat.

Down on the Factory Farm

Micro-chicks Most factory-farm animals live in cramped conditions. Battery hens lay 90% of the eggs we eat but are 'eggstraordinarily' squashed. It's common to have five hens living in a space the size of a microwave oven!

This Little Piggy Pigs used to live in the wild, pigging out on nuts, insects and any other yummies they could root out. Today, you're more likely to see poor old porkers packed together indoors. In fact, by nature pigs are intelligent, freedom-loving animals – and they're just as friendly and sociable as dogs.

Grounded Gobblers In the wild turkeys can fly at 50 mph, but those raised on factory farms for Christmas dinners are too fat and weak to fly at all.

What, No Pension? Factory-farm animals don't grow old gracefully and retire. They're whisked away to make bacon butties and burgers when they are still young. Often, the animals are injected with growth hormones to make them grow quicker and bigger. Bigger animals means more meat and more money for the factory-farm owners.

Think of all the fun you'd miss out on if you went from being nine to ninety in one year. When a factory-farm animal is injected with hormones, it's like making a tiny baby grow a huge hairy beard while it's still in nappies!

What's the Alternative?

Free-range farms might not make such huge profits for their owners, but they're a happier, more humane alternative to factory farms.

Free-range Hens can fluff their feathers and strutt their stuff in the fresh air. No more battery hen blues!

Free-range Porkers are perkier than their factory-farm cousins. The sows are allowed to suckle their young properly and the piglets play piggy in the middle until they've grown up naturally.

Become a Free-range Shop Detective Grab a magnifying glass and move over Sherlock Holmes . . . here comes the Free-range Detective to perform a supermarket sweep.

There are plenty of products to look out for which give clues about how the animals have been treated. Next time you're out shopping, keep your eyes peeled for some of these products:

Free-range chickens Remember, free-range chickens get their kicks in the open air.

Free-range eggs Only 10% of the eggs we eat come from these hens.

Free-range bacon The rashers can't rush about outside, but the pigs they come from used to.

RSPCA-monitored pork These pigs will definitely have been well cared for.

Organic milk It comes from cows which graze on pastures that have not been sprayed with pesticides.

Why not make a list of what's available in your local supermarket?

21

Bombard Your Burgers with Questions Check out on the ingredients of everything you eat. You may find your burgers include mysterious things like 'mechanically-recovered chicken meat'! 'Pork' or 'beef' sausages sometimes contain strange stuff called 'other meat'.

If you're buying an extra-large chicken, ask yourself, 'Did it get this big naturally?'

Beware of Free-range Frauds! Always question what the packaging **really** means. 'Country Fresh' doesn't mean the same as 'Free Range'. If you can, check the small print – on some so-called free-range farms, hundreds of hens are squashed onto a tiny bit of land so that they're just as cramped as they would be in cages.

Oh my Cod!

In recent times, catching cod has turned into a very fishy business. Too many trawlers have meant that fish stocks are dangerously low in some of the world's fishing areas. If we don't stop catching cod at the present rate, there may be none left in the North Sea in five years' time.

Imagine the scene a few years from now. You go down to the chippy on Friday night for fish and chips twice and are told: 'Sorry mate, they're extinct. You'll have to try another planet!'

Quiz that Kipper! Before you tuck into your next fish finger, try to find out how it was caught. Some fishing methods often harm other sea creatures. Drift nets, up to 40 km long, trap dolphins, sharks, seals and porpoises, as well as the fish we want to eat. Any creature unlucky enough to swim into such a net has probably had its chips. Look out for products like 'dolphin-friendly' tuna, which is caught by fishermen who take care not to trap dolphins in their nets.

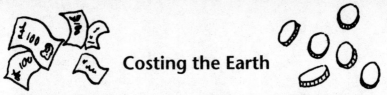

Costing the Earth

We all know that humans pollute the earth. But have you thought that farm animals – especially cattle and factory-farm animals – can cause pollution too? Animals reared for cheap meat need food, water and warmth, and use up valuable natural resources.

In some countries, especially in South America, huge tracts of rainforest are being destroyed to provide land for cattle.

More land is used to grow crops to feed the animals.

Water is needed for the animals to drink, and to irrigate the land which grows animal fodder.

Fossil fuels (coal, gas and oil) are burnt to keep factory-farm animals warm. Processing meat (to make burgers, for example) also uses up fossil fuels.

Manure from factory farms is difficult to get rid of. It may pollute streams and the soil if it is not treated properly.

Methane gas pollutes the air and causes changes in the atmosphere which may lead to global warming. About 20% of total methane output comes from the world's cattle (and it's not caused by cows on motorbikes . . .). More cattle means more methane.

You may find that your cheap burgers are actually costing the earth!

Live Animal Exports

You might think that taking animals abroad would make a nice break from the factory farm. But alas, these trips are not package holidays to Benidorm. Cows, calves, sheep and pigs are squashed into trucks for journeys lasting up to 50 hours. They don't even get let out to go to the loo at the motorway services! Nobody cares about the animals' conditions because they are slaughtered once they arrive at their destination.

The Good News Public pressure can work! Some ferry companies have stopped transporting live animals because of the campaigns against it. If you want to find out about campaigns to halt live animal exports, the following organizations can help.

Compassion in World Farming
5a Charles Street
Petersfield
Hants GU32 3EH

VIVA
(Vegetarians' International Voice for Animals)
PO Box 212
Crewe CW1 4SD

Three

BLOOD SPORTS:
A BLOT ON THE LANDSCAPE?

Whilst out in the countryside, you may have noticed those jolly country types riding horses with packs of dogs. Well, they're not just out having exercise. You may have been witnessing a bout of:

Horses, Hounds and Humans vs. Foxes, Deer and Mink

As if animals didn't have enough problems already (remember Watership Down?), some humans enjoy hunting animals – just for fun!

What Happens at a Hunt?

Specially trained packs of hounds are used to hunt foxes, deer, hares and mink. The hounds are bred to have extra stamina so that they run faster and longer than their prey.

Flabby, unfit foxes should take note and enroll at a Mr Muscles gym before the next hunt.

Fox Hunts Imagine you're at home watching TV, when suddenly forty people on horseback with a pack of hounds crash through your front door and start chasing your dad down the street. It might sound hilarious, but it does really happen to foxes, and it's not their idea of fun.

Foxes may be cunning, but they're usually not cunning enough to outwit a hunting party. It's no game of tag, either. Like James Bond, the hounds have a licence to kill, and when they catch up with the fox, they use it.

Think Mink 'What's a mink?' you ask. 'Is it a mouse with a wink?' No, minks are related to weasels and stoats, and are hunted just like foxes.

Deer, oh Deer Not surprisingly, deer will go to great lengths to escape a hunt. The chase can last up to seven hours, with desperate animals even swimming out to sea or crashing through farms and gardens. (So don't be surprised if you find a deer hiding under your stairs!) The sport ends when the deer is shot. Hmmm. Very sporting.

Hare Hunting Not your dad's lost toupé, but floppy-eared animals who have to leap for their lives when the hunt is in town. Just as your dad's hair might be getting rarer, so are hares in the wild.

Hare hunting gone mad

The Great Hunting Debate

Animal rights activists (and many other people) would like to see hunting banned. It's a big debate, and you'll hear several arguments in favour of hunting. These are some common questions about hunting (also called blood sports) along with the way that anti-hunt campaigners usually reply to them:

Aren't foxes a threat to farmers' chickens?
About 90% of all chickens are cooped up in factory farms, and only the craftiest of foxes could pull off a daring raid against battery hens. However, a few free-range chickens do get chomped by foxes.

Doesn't hunting help to control (or cull) the deer, fox and mink populations?
Only a small percentage of these animals are killed by hunting. If necessary, they could be killed much more humanely and efficiently.

well, we had to control the numbers you know!

Isn't hunting a great traditional English sport?
Well, it used to be traditional to send six-year-olds up chimneys.

Tradition sucks!

Does hunting help to conserve the countryside?
Riding through the countryside like a turbo-charged Dick Turpin can actually cause damage to crops and land. Fox-hungry hounds may also harm other animals during the hunt.

What a drag! It might sound as though anti-hunt campaigners just want to spoil everyone else's fun. But you can get the thrill of the chase without the frightened foxes. Drag hunting uses horses and hounds to chase a person who leaves a scent (dragging it along with them). The person survives, the hounds are rewarded and everyone is happy.

A Job For Life?

Life's not all that hunky-dory for the hunt animals either. . . How would the horses and hounds feel if they knew that:

• Hounds, unlike famous football players, don't become sports commentators when they pass peak fitness. Hunting hounds retire when they are five to seven-years-old, and are often put to sleep.

• Hounds are not taught the Green Cross Code, and are sometimes killed as they run across busy roads or railway lines.

• If a hunt becomes hectic, it's not unusual for a horse to be injured. A hunt rider may even get through several horses in one season.

we demand shorter hours and a real pension plan!

Start Scribbling!

Where does hunting take place? On huge country estates owned by Sir Nathan Dribblethwaite III? Sometimes . . . but it often happens on public land too. Many local councils have already banned hunting on their land. Has yours? Why not find out?

Miss Frieda Fox,
10 Deer Drive,
Foxhuntingdon,
FOX 1CU

Foxhuntingdon Borough Council,
Town Hall,
Foxhuntingdon,
FOX TROT

Dear Sir/Madam,

I am writing to ask whether hunting is still permitted on council-owned land. Some councils have already banned it, and I would like to know what the situation is in the Foxhuntingdon area.

Yours faithfully,

Frieda Fox

Other Blood Sports

Even without the help of horses and hounds,
humans still indulge in other kinds of hunting.
What do you think about these 'sports'?

Hare Coursing Like greyhound racing, but dogs chase a real
hare instead of a fake one.

Bullfighting Spanish bulls certainly see red when a matador's in
town. Bulls are taunted by the matador and killed with swords.

Shooting Birds Clay pigeons don't grumble when you shoot
them out of the sky. Real birds aren't so keen on this sport, though.

Forgotten Fish Do you think fishing is just a harmless
pastime for off-duty vicars? Fish may feel differently. A slippery
salmon is not as cuddly as Fido or Tiddles, but, like other
animals, fish have a central nervous system and can feel pain.

But don't despair! Things are looking up! Some kinds of hunting are already illegal.

Badgering the Badger Baiters Badger baiting is against the law. It involves sending dogs into a badger's sett (or burrow) to make the animals fight. Not a friendly gesture!

Even though it's illegal, badger baiting still goes on. The good news is that you don't have to be a super hero to beat this cruel pastime. If you hear of it happening near you, just contact the RSPCA or the police.

If you want to give badgers even more help by monitoring their setts, contact:

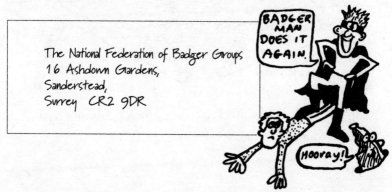

The National Federation of Badger Groups
16 Ashdown Gardens,
Sanderstead,
Surrey CR2 9DR

What Else Can You Do?

You could get in touch with an organization called **The League Against Cruel Sports**. It has many local groups that could use extra campaigners like yourself. You might help on a street stall giving out information, or raise funds with an activity like a sponsored spaghetti suck (or something-or-other).

Petitions Signing a petition against hunting is a short and simple way of showing support. Your squiggly signature goes with thousands of others and shows the people in power what Joe Public really thinks. The pen can be mightier than the shotgun.

Better still, send off for your own petition forms and pass them round everyone you know.

Leaflets Send off for some anti-hunting leaflets, get out your felt-tips and make a stylish dispenser, and ask if you can put them in your school, library or doctor's waiting room. They'll make a change from reading old copies of *Tooth Ache Weekly* next time you go to the dentist.

Clearing Up Whenever you're near a river or lake, watch out for old, abandoned fishing tackle. Pick it up (carefully) and put it in a dustbin (wrapped in old newspaper if there are any sharp edges). Old fishing tackle can injure birds and other wildlife.

Talking Point Ask your teacher if you can discuss blood sports in class- perhaps have a debate.

These addresses can help with information:

Animal Freedom,
PO Box 370a
Surbiton,
Surrey KT6 4YN

The League Against Cruel Sports,
83/87 Union Street,
London SE1 1SG

37

More Scribbling!

If you've not yet got writer's cramp, you can compose letters about hunting to your MP and the local paper. MPs can vote whichever way they like about issues such as hunting, and you'd be surprised how many people read the local paper. If you want to be right on, write on.

Miss Anne T. Hunting,
10 Terrier Walk,
Dunhuntingdon
BNO 1SEY

Dunhuntingdon Gazette,
Newsprint Towers,
Dunhuntingdon
SAY 1T

Dear Dunhuntingdon Gazette,

I am writing to say how strongly opposed to fox hunting I am. Why does such a cruel sport exist in our civilized society? Most people would like to see it banned, tradition or no tradition. We shall be collecting signatures for our anti-hunting petition outside Dunhuntingdon Town Hall next Saturday. I hope your readers will sign it and help to save the foxes.

Yours sincerely,

Anne T. Hunting

Spread the word, hunting's absurd!

Four
ANIMALS IN THE LAB

Should rabbits wear make-up?

Do dogs smoke cigarettes?

They don't usually, but they do in over 400 research laboratories in Britain.

Using animals for scientific research is called 'animal testing' or 'vivisection', and altogether, an estimated 3 million animals were used in scientific experiments last year. At best, these experiments are uncomfortable; at worst they are deadly. Mice are often injected with diseases and then given new drugs to see if they cure them. Other animals may have chemicals dropped in their eyes or have substances rubbed on their skin to see what happens.

Is it Really Necessary?

Many scientists believe that we could never have developed some of our modern life-saving medicines and treatments without animal tests. Every animal activist has to decide for him or herself if they think that the suffering to animals in experiments is justified by the benefits to humans of the results. If you catch a little-known disease (let's call it Mongolian Mugwump Flu) and the only cure is one which had to be tested on animals, you might well decide, on balance, that those tests were a good thing.

However, medical experiments are not the only tests that make use of animals. Do you think these other types of scientific research are quite so important or beneficial?

Cosmetics Companies are always looking for new cosmetics, perfumes, shampoos and deodorants to launch into our already-crowded chemists shops. All these products must be tested to make sure they are safe for humans to use.

Food Additives Chemicals that help to preserve the food we eat or make it look or taste better.

Weapons Animals have been used to test new weapons (which can then be used to kill people!)

Space Research In some countries monkeys have boldly gone where no man has gone before, never to return!

Alternative Remedies

Often, doing experiments on animals is not even a very good way of testing a new drug or chemical (it's certainly never the only way). Humans and animals may react to the same substances in very different ways. For example, penicillin can be deadly for guinea pigs, but is a life-saver for humans.

In fact, many of the most eminent scientists and animal activists agree about vivisection: the best thing we can do is to find alternative ways of testing drugs and chemicals.

Spot the Difference Wine and beer make humans behave in strange ways, but rats break down alcohol much more quickly when they drink it, and can not get drunk. So you won't see guzzling rodents falling out of pubs at closing time acting silly.

The Good News Because we are finding newer and better ways of conducting research, the number of animal experiments is falling.

Human Cell Cultures Have you ever looked through a microscope at an onion cell squashed onto a slide in the biology lab at school? Humans, though not onion flavoured, are made up of cells in just the same way. These cells can now be grown in a test tube or a culture dish, and plenty of revealing research can be carried out on them.

Studying People Many diseases are connected to our human lifestyles, so that studying human behaviour is the only way to really understand the disease. Heart disease is a good example. To find a cure with animals, you'd have to use a rabbit who smoked, drank, ate fast food, didn't exercise and got stressed out by their boss at work. Even Einstein couldn't do that in a laboratory!

Computer Simulations There is life after Ninja Warriors for computers – you can use them for more than just Nintendo fun and games. With the right information programmed, computers can predict the effects that a new drug will have on humans.

The Humane Research Trust More good news. This organization has opened a laboratory at the University of East Anglia, dedicated to non-animal testing. It's a small step for animals and a giant leap for laboratory kind!

With All This Good News, What Use Am I?

Experiments without animals don't just spring out of thin air. A lot of funding for them comes from charity. An organization such as ANIMATE (part of the Humane Research Trust) could use your help.

Dig through those old sweaters your gran knitted you, and delve into that dusty toy box. You could have a jumble sale to raise funds for animal-friendly testing.

I support these people - they helped my dad.

ANIMATE,
29 Bramhall Lane South,
Bramhall
SK7 2DN

Be an Animal-Free Shopper Are you a cool customer? Do you take a cruelty-free cruise round the aisles of your local supermarket? Next time you go shopping, take a checklist and find out which products are animal-friendly and which are not. Products not tested on animals usually say so on the packaging.

Products	Brands Not Tested On Animals
COSMETICS	
PERFUMES	
SOAPS	
SHAMPOOS	
TOOTHPASTE	
DEODORANTS	
HOUSEHOLD CLEANERS	
WASHING POWDERS	
BUBBLE BATHS	
SKIN CREAMS	
TISSUE PAPER	
SUN-TAN LOTION	

For a groovy guide to animal-free shopping, write to:

Naturewatch Trust,
Austen House,
122 Bath Road,
Cheltenham,
Glos. GL53 7JX

Think Thank-you Letters Now's your chance to thank someone for something useful. Support companies who do not do tests on animals, and encourage them to extend their range of products.

Mr Mike Up,
10 Deodorant Drive,
Naturefield,
OK 2USE

Nice to Mice Products Ltd.,
Shampoo Towers,
Pleasant Street,
Cosmeticton,
N1CE 2U

Dear Sir/Madam,

I am writing to thank you for your new cruelty-free skin creams. I am always keen to support companies who do not test their products on animals. I hope that you will extend your range of cosmetics in the future.

Yours faithfully,

Mike Up

If you want to get nasty with companies which still test on animals, punish them with your customer power. Write and tell them that you won't be buying their products in the future.

Mr Mike Up,
10 Deodorant Drive,
Naturefield,
OK 2USE

Ruthless to Rabbits Plc.,
Chemical Buildings,
Bleach Street,
Cosmeticton,
BAD 4U

Dear Sir/Madam,

I am writing to inform you that from now on I shall no longer be buying any of your products unless you stop testing on animals. There are many alternatives to animal testing and other companies are already using them. I shall also be asking my friends to boycott your goods.

Yours faithfully,

Mike Up

Dissection at School

Remember what they say in your first biology lesson: 'Biology is the study of life.' You don't *have* to dissect animals to see how they live.

Dissection may not be compulsory at your school, and there are many good alternatives (including computer simulations and videos that will take you on a journey inside a rat's body).

However, if your school does still practice dissection, and you want to protest against it, ask your parents to raise the issue at the Parent/Teacher Association. You could also contact the Anti-Vivisection Society for an information pack on the ins and outs of dissection.

The National Anti-Vivisection Society,
51 Harley Street,
London W1

Five
ZOOS: CONSERVATION OR CRUELTY?

Taking a trip to the zoo may be fun for you, but how much do the animals enjoy it? Being a zoo animal is a 24-hour job – unlike you, the animals can't go home at the end of the day to roam in their natural habitat.

On the other hand, zoos can teach us a great deal about animals, which in turn may help us to protect endangered species. So what are the pros and cons in the great zoo debate . . ?

Too Close For Comfort Many animals are not used to being close to humans and may find it disturbing. (If you think your family are strange, imagine how they must seem to the average polar bear!

It's a Jungle Out There We humans are quite happy to open a can of beans when we're hungry, but it's different for wild animals. When they're not finding lunch themselves, they are busy avoiding being someone else's lunch.

In zoos, wild animals are fed and protected from predators, and they can get bored and frustrated.

Lonely Lions Some animals need to get together with their own kind. In zoos, naturally sociable animals are sometimes left without family or friends, and feel isolated and confused.

Bored Bears Go Barmy Because they can't lead natural lives, zoo animals run the risk of developing abnormal behaviour patterns. Repetitive pacing, rocking from side to side and biting the bars are all signs that an animal may be suffering from 'zoochosis' (not a new pop group, but a brainy scientific term to describe this sad behaviour).

It's Not All Boos To Zoos

The good news is that zoos can play a very valuable role in research and conservation. Some animals would actually be extinct without their help. The Hawaiian goose, Pere David's deer and the Golden Lion tamarin may all have disappeared without the help of zoo breeding programmes.

If only dinosaurs had discovered zoos before it was too late.

A Success Story Golden Lion tamarins are beautiful beasts, battling for survival in the steamy but disappearing rainforests of Brazil. They have been successfully bred in captivity and then released into the wild. Back in their natural habitat, not all of them survived, but the project did manage to increase the total number of animals by 25-30%.

Going Wild Helping animals to readapt to life in the wild after being in captivity is usually the hardest part of zoo breeding programmes. You know how it is – just like readapting to school after the lazy summer holidays!

The Great Debate

What do your friends and teachers think about zoos? Why not ask your teacher to organize a class debate about zoos. These are some of the questions you could talk about:

Should money for zoos be spent on other things, such as preserving animals in the wild or funding anti-poaching patrols?

Can we learn anything from seeing real animals close up in zoos that we can not learn from books or films?

Is it worth saving animals from extinction if they're going to live in a zoo all their lives?

You can get further information on the pros and cons of zoos from these two organizations:

The Born Free Foundation
Coldharbour,
Dorking
Surrey RH5 6HA

Wildlife Dept,
RSPCA Headquarters,
Causeway,
Horsham,
West Sussex RH1 1HG

Zoos, You, and What to Do

Freeing all the animals in every zoo in Britain probably won't help them that much. Neither will asking your mum if they can come and live round at your house.

On the other hand, zoos do vary enormously in the quality of care and conditions that they give to the animals. Some provide much better homes than others. Good zoos make sure that monkeys have room to swing around and the penguins space to swim.

Next time you visit a zoo, take a good critical look. Make a quick questionnaire for each of the animals, carefully read the information boards next to the enclosures and ask yourself some questions about the conditions of the animals.

Watch out for bored bears and cramped camels! Take it away Zoo Detective. . .

SPECIES: Elephant

Is the enclosure big enough? Elephant house is small, but there is a big exercise yard for warm weather.

Does the enclosure resemble the animal's natural habitat? Not really.

Would the animal normally live alone or in a group? In a group.

Is the animal behaving normally?

Could you improve the enclosure? How?

If you think any improvements are necessary at the zoo you visit, write to the owners and let them know.

Miss Anne M.L. Cage,
10 Wildlife Gardens,
Zootopia,
ZOO 1SBAD

Mr Z Keeper,
Alcatraz Animal Park,
Alcatraz Island,
NOS CAPE

Dear Mr Keeper,

I am writing to say how disappointed I felt when I visited your zoo last week. I noticed that many animals did not have enough space to move about properly, and some of the sociable animals (such as the monkeys) were living by themselves. I have written to the RSPCA to check on their requirements for living space for wild animals in zoos, and I shall not be visiting your zoo again.

Yours sincerely,

Anne M.L. Cage

Six

THE ANIMAL
ENTERTAINMENT SWINDLE

Think of how often you watch animals performing, in films, on TV or even in the street. Seeing cute animals doing human-type things is always guaranteed to raise a giggle, and even the hardest he-man's heart melts when he watches Lassie coming home.

Scenes such as these might be heartwarming for humans, but they are not necessarily such fun for the performing animals involved.

The Big Flop

Behind the shine of the greasepaint and the roar of the crowd, circus animals have to do things that would make even the curliest lion-tamer's moustache straighten out in surprise.

Strange Behaviour Circus animals are made to behave unnaturally, which must seem puzzling or disturbing. What's more, before they strut their stuff in the ring, these animals spend most of their time locked in cages or tethered by chains.

On The Road Elephants may be used to roaming for miles in the wild, but zooming up and down the M1 on the back of a lorry is no fun at all. Being a circus animal means a lot of travelling in a restricted space.

Daring Lion Tamers? Animal trainers may be more cruel than courageous because they use whips, sticks (and fear) to teach tricks to their wild animals.

How would you like it if you were locked in your bedroom all day with a broken TV, no walkman and a shelf full of books you'd read ten times before? The only time you are let out for an hour is to jig through rings of fire to entertain your Great Aunt Gertrude.

Putting a Stop to the Big Top

If you would prefer Nellie the Elephant to pack her trunk and say goodbye to the circus, stop going to them yourself. Or choose a modern, animal-free circus where humans are the only creatures to perform death-defying stunts.

You can get more information about performing animals and how they are protected by sending a SAE to the RSPCA (address on p55).

As with fox hunting, many local councils have now banned circuses with animals from their land, so you could write to your council to make sure that in your district the show goes on elsewhere. Or why not put more pressure on your MP?

When they're not shouting 'hear, hear' in parliament or opening village fetes, MPs can make new laws. Tell yours if you think that animal circuses make as much sense as quadruple trigonometry and should be banned.

Anne T. Circus,
10 Trapeze Corner,
Dumbton,
BAN 1T

Mr Ringo Fire MP,
House of Commons,
London SW1A 0AA

Dear Mr Fire,

I am writing about my concern for the welfare of circus animals. I think using animals for entertainment in this way is cruel and unnecessary. Making the circus animals do silly tricks teaches us nothing about wildlife and many animals live in very poor conditions. Please support legislation to make animal circuses illegal and end this pointless tradition.

Yours sincerely,

Anne T. Circus

Disappearing Dolphinariums

Dolphinariums are 'water circuses' where dolphins and whales are made to do tricks (like jumping through hoops). Animal rights groups in Britain were jumping through hoops for joy in 1994 when they realized that their campaigns to close down this country's dolphinariums had been successful.

Whales and dolphins are highly intelligent animals who can't be fooled. A swimming pool just isn't so much fun as the whole ocean.

However, whales and dolphins still need our help in the wild – if you want more information on how to really make a dolphin smile, contact:

The Whale & Dolphin
Conservation Society,
Alexander House,
James Street West,
Bath BA1 2BT

Making a Killing on the Gee-Gees

Having the odd flutter on the Grand National might seem harmless enough, but every year horses are injured or even put to sleep after breaking their legs jumping high fences. If you think your dad's sneaking off to put a couple of quid on a 'nice little earner', ask him to think again.

There are fewer injuries involved in snail racing. Why not try that instead (the fun lasts much longer . . .)

A PG Tip For Everyone Chimpanzees don't really drink tea and live in chintzy sitting rooms in Sidcup. Television often gives you a misleading view of wildlife behaviour.

You've Been Framed!

If you're soaking up the rays on the Costa Del Ot, watch out for men with monkeys and parrots who are hoping to make some 'pieces of eight'. Before you have your photo taken with their animals, here are a few thoughts:

Are the animals being properly cared for?

What do the animals get out of this?

My little brother's a cheeky monkey. Maybe I should get my photo taken with him instead?

It's usually best to avoid having your photo taken with exotic animals as they're often mistreated by their owners.

Seven
CREATURE COMFORTS – PETS AT HOME

when I was a lad...

Like charity, animal activism begins at home – or it should. Every day, over 1,000 animals are put down because their owners don't want them (or can't look after them) any longer. So, before you buy a pet think hard about whether you can give it a good, happy home for the rest of its life. A puppy or a kitten can live for over 15 years. That's a lot of rubber mice and walkies.

Can I Give My Pet a Good Home?

Enough Space? There's a big difference between keeping a pet spider in a matchbox and a pet camel in a block of flats. Some animals need a lot of space, so ask yourself if your home is big enough for them. Will your pet need a garden to play in?

One of the Family Will the more squeamish members of your family take kindly to your housing a boa constrictor in your bedroom? It helps if your new pet gets on with the rest of the family.

Enough Time? Between going to school, slaving over your homework and going to the quantum physics and trainspotting footballers' cookery club, is there time to pamper your poodle? (Don't forget, your parents won't have time to clean out the hamster cage either.) All pets need exercise, feeding and regular cleaning or grooming. Some pets (like dogs) need training too. These things all take up time.

Sadly, dogs can not be trained to eat homework.

Two's Company Some animals, like rabbits, are sociable and need the company of other animals. However, you must be careful not to mix males and females, or you'll be overrun by baby bunnies!

How Much is That Doggy in the Window?

Probably more than you think. . . All pets cost money, not just to buy, but also to keep. Some are much more expensive than others – an average dog can quite easily cost £1,000 a year. Make a checklist and work out how much the animal you want will cost to keep for a year. Remember to include:

Food Find out how much your pet will need to eat.

Vaccinations Dogs and cats must be vaccinated each year by a vet.

Neutering Dogs and cats should be neutered by the vet so that they can not have babies. It costs about £100, but the RSPCA recommends that all dogs and cats are neutered (unless they will be used for breeding). Otherwise, thousands of unwanted pups and kittens have to be put down each year.

Pet Accessories Depends on the pet, but you will need some of the following: a cage; a collar; a basket and blanket; a lead.

Holidays If you go on holiday, you may have to pay someone to look after your pet while you're away.

BYE

Vets' Bills A single trip to the vet will cost at least £15. Most people take out annual health insurance for their pet.

Animal-friendly Action

Animal Rescue Centres Pet shops are always brimming over with cute, bright-eyed animals, but before you buy, stop and think. There are many other unwanted pets in animal rescue centres who would be chuffed to bits to come and live with you for free.

For information on animal rescue centres near you, contact the RSPCA at the address on page 55.

Animal Sanctuaries If you decide you can't really look after a pet full time, why not volunteer to help out at an animal sanctuary? These centres look after a host of abandoned or mistreated animals from rabbits and geese to donkeys and dogs. Make a donkey's day with your leftover carrots!

Walking the Dog If you're a petless person you could also offer your services as a potential pedigree perambulator (or dog walker). Some people (especially the elderly) may not be able to exercise their dogs as much as they'd like. With your parents' permission, you could put an advert in your local shop window.

Can you never find enough time to rove with Rover?

Could you use someone (top speed 5 mph) to walk your dog?

All pooches considered, from poodles to pekinese.

Please leave details with newsagent.

The RSPCA Saves the Day

The Royal Society for the Prevention of Cruelty to Animals is the world's oldest animal welfare association. When it's not taking care of abandoned animals, it's prosecuting animal abusers or trying to change laws about animals.

Humble Origins The RSPCA was formed on 16 June 1824, when a gathering of distinguished figures met at Ye Old Slaughters Coffee House. They wanted to reduce the cruelty to animals they saw going on around them.

Royal Seal of Approval Queen Victoria gave the RSPCA her royal approval in 1840. Since then, the association has become a British institution.

Reporting Animal Cruelty Sadly, cruelty to animals still goes on today, almost two centuries after the RSPCA was founded. If you see an act of cruelty, keep your wits about you. Try to remember details of what happened, such as names, addresses, times, dates, places or car registration numbers. You can then report the incident to the RSPCA. They will do all they can to stop it happening again.

The RSPCA receives about a million calls every year, so you won't be the only person aware of cruelty to animals.

Eight
GOING VEGGIE

Does the word 'vegetarian' make you cringe? Do you dread the prospect of endless nut roasts and lentil casseroles? Have you heard stories about mad Uncle Quentin who went veggie and was trapped for ever in a world of home-brewed nettle beer, astrological beard yoga and mung bean salads?

In fact, it's not just a load of old hippies who become vegetarian nowadays. Thousands of normal people stop eating meat (or eat less meat) every week. . .

Famous Veggies The Buddha was a budding veggie as far back as 500 BC. Today, Damon Albarn (of Blur) and Jason Orange (of Take That) are both vegetarians. And if eating lettuces doesn't sound much of a laugh, think again, because Victoria Wood and Joanna Lumley have both switched from sausages to celery. There are plenty of other carrot-crunching celebrities around – and a few of your friends and relations may well be veggie too.

Do you know any other famous vegetarians? List them here:

Vegetarian Hall of Fame

Staying Healthy

So what *do* vegetarians really eat? In fact, there's a huge variety of tasty veggie nosh – and even if your tastebuds still tingle for the taste of meat, you can always buy veggie burgers, sausages, shepherd's pies and bacon to satisfy those carnivorous cravings.

A Well-balanced Diet Just because you're not eating meat doesn't mean you can live off cheese and onion crisps. If you do decide to go vegetarian, you must make sure that nutrients from meat are replaced by other foods. However, a good, well-balanced vegetarian diet is actually better than a meat-based one (it has less saturated fats and more dietary fibre).

The Vegetarian Society can give sound advice on a healthy vegetarian diet.

The Vegetarian Society,
Parkdale,
Dunham Road,
Altrincham,
Cheshire WA14 4QD

Protein Power If you tell your parents that you're going veggie, they may quake with fear and mumble that you won't get enough protein. That's the stuff you need for growth, tissue repair and protection against infections.

Don't worry! Protein lurks in every corner of a sussed-out vegetarian's plate. Guzzle these foods and the protein pangs will be kept at bay!

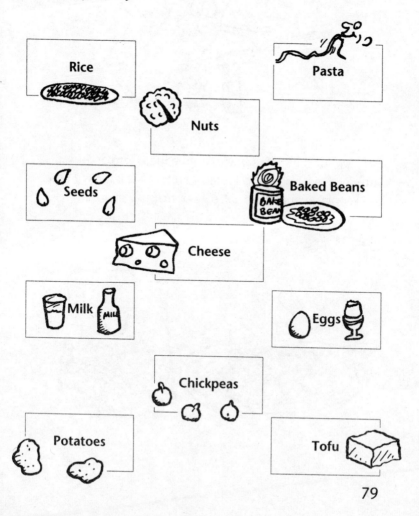

Rice

Pasta

Nuts

Seeds

Baked Beans

Cheese

Milk

Eggs

Chickpeas

Potatoes

Tofu

Tofu No, this isn't an ancient Chinese method of vegetarian kung-fu, but a protein-rich product made from soya beans. It usually comes in chunks, and if you cook it properly (with a fave flavouring), tofu will become a treat for your taste buds.

Hiiyaaa!

TVP Or, for those of you who want a more formal introduction, 'Textured Vegetable Protein'. This looks a little bit like mince, and if you spice it up, makes a smashing spaghetti bolognese.

T.V.P.

Vital Vitamins Vitamins keep us healthy and protect us from illnesses like heart disease. The good news for vegetarians is that fruit and vegetables abound in vitamins. They are also found in other veggie staples, such as wholemeal bread, beans, nuts and yeast extract.

Calcium Your mum might worry that your teeth will fall out and your bones will shrink if you stop eating meat. Put her mind at ease and tell her that leafy green vegetables, dairy products, nuts and seeds all provide plenty of calcium. Spinach is a good source – look what it did for Popeye!

Iron You don't have to eat a mini-metro sandwich to get more iron. It's found in baked beans, wholemeal bread, leafy green vegetables, dried fruit and lentils.

Consuming Carbohydrates Adults are always talking about energy conservation and getting you to switch off the lights. Now you can fight back with a bit of energy consumption! Carbohydrates are our main source of energy and can be found in fruit, milk, sugar, wheat, rice, pasta, lentils, potatoes and nuts, to name but a few.

Dietary Fibre This is also known as 'roughage' and is contained in fruits and wholemeal bread. It acts like your body's caretaker, sweeping away poisons and cleaning out your insides.

Now you know what foods to eat, how about a simple secret vegetarian delicacy . . ?

Les Haricots sur Pain Grillé

1   Carefully open a tin of baked beans and heat gently in a saucepan.

2   Select two of the finest slices of bread (white or brown according to taste), place in a toaster and cook until golden brown.

3   Artistically arrange the beans on the toast. (Make sure the toast is on a plate first to avoid unnecessary mess.)

Et voilà! Beans on toast, a healthy vegetarian meal.

Parental Persuasion

So you're going to become a vegetarian, with a healthier diet. Your mum will be tickled pink, won't she?

Even the most understanding parents will find a vegetarian child a bit of an inconvenience (extra shopping, special meals, etc., etc.), so here are some top tips from our 'Convince-A-Mum' Campaign.

Start by telling your parents that a well-balanced veggie diet is healthier for you. You won't need so much time off school for illness, will learn more and thus become mega-brainy!

Mum, I'm going veggie!

Oh no!

Go shopping and point out that there are now loads of vegetarian convenience foods.

Start doing the washing up.

Buy your mum some flowers.

Tell your dad that a veggie diet can be cheaper. The money he saves on shopping can go towards a holiday in the Carribean.

Buy a vegetarian cookery book and dazzle the family by being a whizz in the kitchen.

Being a Veggie Shopper

If you've already tried your hand at being a Free-range Detective, why not prowl the supermarket as an Ingredients Investigator too?

Many products now have a green 'V' sign on them, telling you that they are suitable for vegetarians. Certain foods, on the other hand, contain hidden animal extras. Watch out for these disguises:

Animal Fat Not such a cunning disguise, but it still tries to hide in cakes and biscuits where you might not be expecting it.

Gelatine Sounds harmless enough, but this is jelly obtained by boiling the skin, tendons, ligaments and bones of animals.

Rennet Usually hides in cheese. It is, in fact, extract from a calf's stomach.

Anchovy If you decide not to eat fish, you'll want to avoid anchovies. They are small members of the herring family.

Cochineal (E120) If you think creepy crawlies should be left to crawl in peace, avoid this food colouring. It is a dye made of dried insects.

Vegetarian Options

Is School Dinner a Winner? Poor old school dinners are always getting picked on. But amongst all the jokes about semolina pudding, vegetarians are often left with a choice of chips, chips or chips. Your school might be progressive and provide good vegetarian alternatives. If not, speak to your teacher or contact the Parent/Teacher Association and say, 'Please provide more than pommes frites!'

Eating Out Because vegetarianism is so popular, lots of restaurants now dish up vegetarian delights by the dozen.

A Dog's Dinner? If you're visiting friends, don't forget that it's good manners (and good sense) to tell them that you're a vegetarian before you arrive. Otherwise you could find your dinner being fed to the dog.

Will one more vegetarian make a difference?

Yes, he or she will! Here's what a meat eater's menu may look like for a lifetime.

GREEDY PIG RESTAURANT

Starters:
5 cows, 20 pigs, 29 sheep and 7 rabbits

Main Course:
760 chickens, 46 turkeys and 15 ducks

Dessert:
one and a half geese and half a tonne of fish

That's a lot of animals!

A vegetarian diet uses up much less farmland than a meat-eater's. Land that provides just two people with meat can provide enough food for 60 vegetarians!

And Then There Were Vegans. . .

Contrary to popular belief, vegans are not outcasts from old episodes of Star Trek. They are people who do not eat any animal products at all, including milk, cheese, butter, eggs and sometimes even honey.

You might think, 'That's illogical, Captain', or you might want to find out more about veganism. It's not easy and you must be extra-careful to eat a balanced diet, so don't try it unless you know what you are doing. On the other hand, many people eat well and live perfectly healthily as vegans.

Munch On! Whatever you decide about eating meat, make sure you have a healthy, balanced diet and don't ever feel inconvenient about asking for vegetables instead of steak. Keep an eye out too for National Vegetarian Week. Something interesting may be happening near you.

Nine
CARRY ON CAMPAIGNING

If you become involved in a local animal rights group, it could lead to all kinds of exciting activities: helping out on a stall, fundraising, collecting signatures for a petition or even putting on your hiking boots and going out on a march.

If you do take part in a demonstration, make sure that you advertise it properly. Hand out fliers, make posters and write to your local newspaper saying where and when the march will take place.

Why not make some banners to tell the world what you think. Can you come up with some snappy slogans such as 'Save the Whale' or 'Hug the Slug' for these animals?

93

Starting Your Own Animal Rights Group

Be your own boss in battling for animal rights.
Starting a group is hard work but once it's off the
ground there'll be no stopping you. A group at school
is a good place to start.

Think of a Name Something like 'Coventry Comprehensive's
Cruelty-Free Animal Club' will do the trick (if you live in
Coventry).

Time and Place Behind the bike sheds during quadruple
physics probably is not the best time and place for your first
meeting. Ask if you can use a room at break or just after school,
and decide at the beginning how often you will have meetings.

Money Will you charge a subscription to pay for paper, stamps and anything else the group will need?

Get Some Support Help from sympathetic teachers will be very valuable. A trustworthy adult will come in handy as a treasurer to look after any money and to help with producing a newsletter.

Making Contacts Write off to your favourite national groups and ask them to send you leaflets, posters and information on any of their campaigns which you could support.

Most important of all, your group will have to choose its first cause to campaign about. What is the first issue you would like to tackle? You should have a few ideas by now. . .

And Finally

Animal rights are everywhere. From trekking through tropical rainforests to save tigers from extinction to snooping through your local zoo, an animal rights activist's work is never done.

Whatever you do, whether it's adopting a whale, campaigning against blood sports or simply eating free-range eggs, you'll be making a difference.

So get out there, and give the animals something to ROAR about, by replacing human wrongs with animal rights.